THE Women OF THE BIBLE Speak

COLORING BOOK

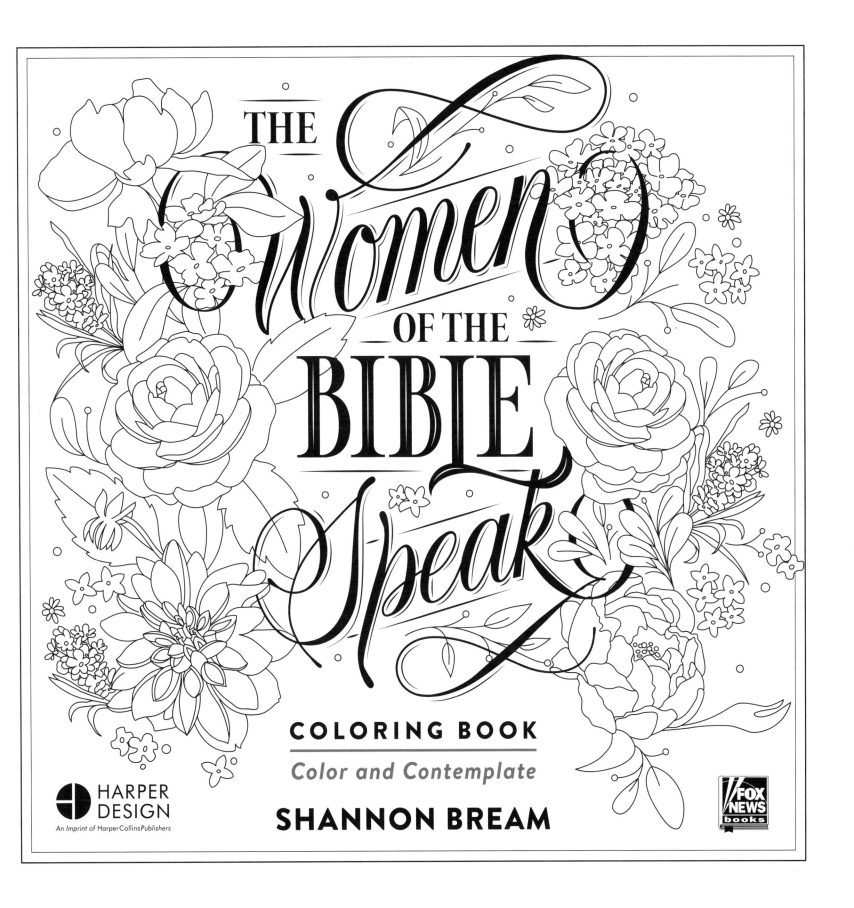

THE Women OF THE BIBLE Speak

COLORING BOOK

Color and Contemplate

HARPER DESIGN
An Imprint of HarperCollins Publishers

SHANNON BREAM

FOX NEWS books

Some material has been previously published in a different format.

HarperCollins books may be purchased for educational, business, or sales promotional use.
For information please email the Special Markets Department at SPsales@harpercollins.com.

Published in 2023 by
Harper Design
An Imprint of HarperCollinsPublishers
195 Broadway
New York, NY 10007
Tel: (212) 207-7000
Fax: (855) 746-6023
harperdesign@harpercollins.com
www.hc.com

Distributed throughout the world by
HarperCollins Publishers
195 Broadway
New York, NY 10007

ISBN 978-0-06-330740-7
Printed in Canada
23 24 25 26 27   10 9 8 7 6 5 4 3 2 1

WELCOME

Throughout the pages of the Bible, God shines a spotlight on the women who were key players in His unfolding plan. Each of the women of the Bible is unique. Consider the warrior's heart of Jael and Deborah, the insight of Sarah and Hagar, the steadfast hope of Rachel and Leah, the devotion of Tamar and Ruth, the quick courage of Esther and Rahab, and the prophetic voice of Miriam and Hannah. Or reflect on how Jesus heralded the life and faith of Mary and Martha of Bethany, Mary Magdalene, and His own beloved mother, Mary of Nazareth.

Some of these women were brave and believers from the start. Others felt overwhelmed by and unsure of the assignment set before them by God. Some had great positions of power, while others were outcasts. Some were devout, while others lived in defeat. Each woman reminds us that it doesn't matter if we view ourselves as weak, inadequate, faithless, or afraid—God always has a plan for us.

Whether you're currently on a sunny mountaintop or trudging through a harrowing valley, God is weaving your story into His greater plan. Through His word, we are pointed to these women, who provide inspiration and encouragement for our own lives.

SARAH

"I will bless those who bless you,
and whoever curses you I will curse;
and all peoples on earth
will be blessed through you."

GENESIS 12:3

Sarah and Abraham struggled to believe God would give them a child. At the announcement that Sarah would become pregnant, the ninety-year-old burst out laughing (Genesis 18:12). She had hoped long enough, tried long enough, and waited long enough that she'd given up hope.

Yet God was gracious to Sarah, and nine months later she gave birth to a son. Sarah became a key player, a "mother of nations" (Genesis 17:16). All the world was blessed through her. Sarah's story reminds us that nothing is impossible with God. Just as the wildly unthinkable finally came true for her, it can for you, too!

Despite our flaws, we can be used by our Heavenly Father
to weave together His highest purposes.

HAGAR

She gave this name to the Lord who spoke to her:
"You are the God who sees me," for she said,
"I have now seen the One who sees me."

GENESIS 16:13

As a maidservant, Hagar was treated like property rather than as a person. She was forced to become Abraham's concubine, and from the moment Hagar became pregnant, she was treated horribly and ran away.

God sent an angel to Hagar because He had seen her suffering. The angel instructed Hagar to return to Sarah and serve her. Through this act of obedience, God would multiply Hagar's descendants greatly (Genesis 16:10).

Hagar said, "You are the God who sees me . . . I have now seen the One who sees me" (Genesis 16:13). No longer overlooked or ignored, Hagar was perfectly seen and known. Her story teaches that when you feel the most invisible, never forget: God's eyes and favor are always on you.

The "God Who Sees" is the God who sees not
with the eyes of the world, but with the eyes of heaven.

RACHEL

Then God remembered Rachel;
he listened to her and enabled her to conceive.

GENESIS 30:22

Rachel experienced a match made in heaven—literally. The moment Jacob saw her, he fell head over heels in love. Everything seemed picture perfect until Laban, Rachel's father, tricked Jacob into marrying Rachel's older sister, Leah. For Jacob, the prescribed time of seven extra years of hard labor to earn Rachel's hand in marriage seemed only but a few days.

While Leah produced children for Jacob, Rachel watched in agony. She obsessed over becoming pregnant, and her jealousy drove her to extreme measures. God eventually gave Rachel many children of her own—not because of her cleverness but because of her fervent prayers—and, rest assured, He hears your prayers too.

What happened in her life so often happens in ours as well.
All of us will experience grief, a loss, or a situation beyond our control.

LEAH

She conceived again, and when she gave birth to a son she said, "This time I will praise the Lord." So she named him Judah. Then she stopped having children.

GENESIS 29:35

Even as the older sister to Rachel, Leah felt that she was always playing second fiddle. While the dazzling Rachel was described as beautiful, undesirable Leah was portrayed as having "weak eyes" (Genesis 29:17). Their father, Laban, had to trick Jacob into marrying her.

God saw her suffering and had great mercy. Leah gave birth to Jacob's first son, Reuben, because of what the Lord had done for her. Then she gave birth to three more: Simeon, because God had "heard" her; Levi, representing her longing to be joined to Jacob; and Judah, where she declared, "I will praise the Lord" (Genesis 29:32–35). Her story reminds us that even in our affliction, God sees us, hears us, and gives us reason to praise Him.

The people who force us to deal with difficult circumstances can also be the ones who push us into a deeper relationship with God.

TAMAR

Judah recognized them and said, "She is more righteous than I, since I wouldn't give her to my son Shelah." And he did not sleep with her again.

GENESIS 38:26

Tamar was given in marriage to Er, and then his brother Onan, both of whom were so awful that God took their lives. The responsibility of caring for Tamar fell on her father-in-law, Judah, but he sent her away. She was left with no hope or future except for being a dependent in her father's house until the day she died. But Tamar refused to give up.

She formulated a plan to expose Judah's failures by tricking him to sleep with her. When Judah realized all the evil that he'd done, he declared, "She is more righteous than I . . " (Genesis 38:26). Through Tamar's courage, she becomes part of the lineage of Jesus Christ, reminding us that God is masterful at making good out of our messes.

God is always working in each of our stories,
able not only to heal us, but also to use
our human frailty to miraculous ends.

RUTH

But Ruth replied, "Don't urge me to leave you or to turn back from you. Where you go I will go, and where you stay I will stay. Your people will be my people and your God my God."

RUTH 1:16

Ruth knew heartache and heartbreak. Her husband and his brother, along with her father-in-law, all died. Ruth, along with her mother-in-law, Naomi, and sister-in-law, Orpah, became a trio of grieving widows with limited prospects for the future.

Rather than become a victim, Ruth made a daring choice to leave everything she knew to follow Naomi into the unknown. "Where you go I will go, and where you stay I will stay" (Ruth 1:16). She soon met Boaz, who married her, and together they built a new life. Naomi, Ruth, and Boaz built a family of choice, a family that branched into the genealogical tree that bears our Savior, reminding us that God specializes in impossible situations.

Even when options seem out of reach,
God is always weaving together the unexpected.

RUTH'S GIFT

The women said to Naomi: "Praise be to the Lord,
who this day has not left you without a guardian-redeemer.
May he become famous throughout Israel!"

RUTH 4:14

Ruth's story is more than just a nice story about a young woman who got her happy ending. Ruth's acceptance into the family of Israel spoke to God's people about their own inclusion into the family of God.

Ruth chose to leave her people and her gods, just as the Gentile people chose to leave theirs. Ruth, like Abraham, became a powerful symbol of the riches that await those who choose to step out in faith and who leave behind the comfortable in favor of the spiritually challenging.

Each of us must listen and be willing when His
unexpected call comes into our lives.

DEBORAH

Then Deborah said to Barak, "Go! This is the day the Lord has given Sisera into your hands. Has not the Lord gone ahead of you?" So Barak went down Mount Tabor, with ten thousand men following him.

JUDGES 4:14

Deborah was a prophetess and judge who governed during some very dark days. She saw the dire situation of her people and decided to act by summoning the warrior, Barak. She instructed him to gather his men at Mount Tabor, along with 10,000 others, because God had planned a victory.

Deborah spoke truth with confidence. She didn't try to minimize the reality of the situation nor try to know all the details. She simply decided to believe in God's faithfulness. She knew God had gone before her—just as He does you. Through her courage, God's people experienced a stunning victory as well as peace throughout the land for decades to come.

It's not up to us, to water down God's perfect plans.
We are simply called to follow His lead and leave the rest up to Him.

DEBORAH'S SONG

The river Kishon swept them away,
the age-old river, the river Kishon.
March on, my soul; be strong!

JUDGES 5:21

Not only was Deborah a powerful leader who oversaw the miraculous overthrow of an enemy oppressing her people; she was also a gifted song writer and worship leader. After the victory, Deborah (along with Barak) recites one of the longest poetic compositions in the Bible. She sings of the history of Israel's wars and the power of God fighting for His people.

The Song of Deborah calls us to praise God and surrender ourselves to Him. It challenges us to remember that we're backed by an unbeatable God. In Him, we can march on no matter what we're facing.

The courage of Deborah is that her
heart was obviously so closely aligned with God's
that she didn't doubt His direction.

JAEL

With God we will gain the victory,
and he will trample down our enemies.

PSALM 108:13

When Deborah instructed Barak to gather his men and go to battle, he hesitated. That reluctance cost Barak a piece of the victory. Deborah prophesied that another female would take out the opposing leader, Sisera. That woman was Jael.

When Sisera arrived at Jael's home, she put him at ease. Then she courageously drove a tent peg through his temple. Jael not only fulfilled one of Deborah's prophecies; she also killed a man who had cruelly oppressed the Israelites for twenty years. Her actions capped off an unexpected, momentous victory of Israel that launched its people into a new era of peace.

In the battles He sets before us,
God expects us to fight as Jael did,
with the weapons we have.

HANNAH

"Not so, my lord," Hannah replied, "I am a woman who is deeply troubled. I have not been drinking wine or beer; I was pouring out my soul to the Lord.

1 SAMUEL 1:15

Hannah ached for a child of her own. To make matters worse, her rival, Peninnah, mocked Hannah for being childless and she was left weeping in despair. She turned to the Lord in her anguish and poured her heart out in prayer. She even made a promise to give up her firstborn son to serve God.

Not long after, Hannah became pregnant and had a son. She named him Samuel, meaning "God has heard." When it comes to prayer, we never need to hold back from God. We can be unafraid to pour out ourselves and know that God hears us and holds us tenderly.

God is always there awaiting our prayers, even when we can't find the words to express our deepest grief.

HANNAH'S FAITH

"Early the next morning they arose and worshiped before the Lord and then went back to their home at Ramah. Elkanah made love to his wife Hannah, and the Lord remembered her."

1 SAMUEL 1:19

God knew every delicate and painful detail of Hannah's life. He saw her grief and longing, her years of heartache, and the cruel insults from others for not being able to have children. God also saw Hannah's faith. Her prayers were so vulnerable and passionate that it drew attention at the tabernacle. Yet Hannah still laid it all on the line. And God remembered Hannah, and she became pregnant.

This mighty woman of faith watched her long-awaited son, Samuel, grow into a great prophet, one who served God and who would one day anoint King David to lead God's people.

God confounds the world by working through people who aren't the strongest or most gifted, directing the glory where it belongs: to Him.

THE

LORD

REMEMBERED

HER

MIRIAM

Therefore we will not fear, though the earth give way and the mountains fall into the heart of the sea.

PSALM 46:2

Pharaoh declared that every Hebrew baby boy born must be tossed into the Nile River to die. But Moses's parents hid their son, refusing to obey the edict. Moses's mother placed him in a basket among the reeds. Miriam, Moses's older sister, stood by to see what might happen.

When young Miriam saw that Pharaoh's daughter had discovered the basket, she stepped forward and offered her own mother to nurse him. Miriam's idea was a move of inspired genius. Through Miriam's bravery, Moses and his mother were reunited, and Moses was positioned to ultimately deliver God's people to freedom. Small acts of courage can change the world.

What would ultimately be the miraculous delivery of His people began with the brave actions of a young girl.

MIRIAM'S SONG

Miriam sang to them:
"Sing to the Lord,
for he is highly exalted.
Both horse and driver
he has hurled into the sea."

EXODUS 15:21

Moses's sister was called "Miriam the Prophetess," a title very few women in the Bible received. After helping save her brother on the bank of the Nile, she watched as God raised Moses to set the Israelites free. An avid supporter of her brother's leadership, she watched God perform miracle after miracle.

After the Israelites crossed the Red Sea, Miriam reached for a timbrel. All the women followed with timbrels and dancing, expressing praise to God. Miriam sang, "Sing to the Lord, for he is highly exalted. Both horse and driver he has hurled into the sea" (Exodus 15:21). Miriam proclaimed God's excellence and faithfulness with joy and celebration. And we can, too!

Moses and all the people have just sung
a much longer song of rejoicing, but it is Miriam who reaches for
a musical instrument to turn all their joy into dance.

ESTHER

For if you remain silent at this time, relief and deliverance for the Jews will arise from another place, but you and your father's family will perish. And who knows but that you have come to your royal position for such a time as this?

ESTHER 4:14

King Xerxes threw a huge party, and when his wife refused to appear, the king hosted a beauty pageant to find a new spouse. Esther won the pageant, yet God was positioning her for something greater.

With the lives of the Jewish people in the balance, Esther discovered she had the influence to save them. Her cousin Mordecai challenged, "And who knows but that you have come to your royal position for such a time as this?" (Esther 4:14). In response, Esther boldly stepped out in faith and saved the Jewish people by appealing to the king. Like Esther, God positions each of us for "such a time as this" moments, too.

We cannot know when He will call us to a task that feels beyond our human limits, but Esther's story is the perfect illustration of how He equips us all along the path that leads us to those moments.

ESTHER'S REQUEST

*"Go, gather together all the Jews who are in Susa,
and fast for me. Do not eat or drink for three days,
night or day. I and my attendants will fast as you do.
When this is done, I will go to the king, even though
it is against the law. And if I perish, I perish."*

ESTHER 4:16

Esther knew that approaching the king uninvited to try to rescue the Jewish people was illegal and punishable by death. So she called together all the Jews for three days of fasting on her behalf. She recognized that this task was larger than she alone could accomplish—and that everything rested on God.

In our moments of great spiritual crisis, we can also reach out to our brothers and sisters from all over the world and find God's power, love, and support unleashed through prayer.

*We don't have to understand physics in order
to know gravity's power, and we don't always have to understand
the mysteries of this amazing gift God has given us, prayer,
to know that it works.*

RAHAB

When we heard of it, our hearts melted in fear and everyone's courage failed because of you, for the Lord your God is God in heaven above and on the earth below.

JOSHUA 2:11

When Joshua's spies showed up at Rahab's front door, she hid them from the king. Soon after, the king sent messengers to Rahab to inquire about the spies. Rahab sent them on a wild-goose chase and then proclaimed her faith to the spies (Joshua 2:11). Following this, Rahab struck a deal with the spies where they would spare her and her family when the armies invaded.

Rahab is the reason that Joshua's army achieved victory in Jericho, and she's even mentioned in Jesus's genealogy. She reminds us that daring acts in a moment of great need can make all the difference.

Like Rahab, we all have to experience a moment when we fully understand the reality of God and His power to redeem us.

MARY OF BETHANY

But few things are needed—or indeed only one.
Mary has chosen what is better,
and it will not be taken away from her.

LUKE 10:42

Mary did two things: she sat at Jesus's feet, and she listened to Him while her sister Martha became overwhelmed from hosting all the guests. When Martha told Jesus that her sister wasn't helping, Jesus defended Mary: "Mary has chosen what is better, and it will not be taken away from her" (Luke 10:42).

In drawing close to Jesus and hanging on His every word, Mary gives us a portrait of how we should approach Jesus with spiritual hunger, knowing that He alone is the One who satisfies our deepest longings.

Mary's story beautifully illustrates the depth of knowing Jesus,
both loving Him with our hearts and intellectually embracing
Him with our minds.

MARTHA OF BETHANY

"Yes, Lord," she replied, "I believe that you are the Messiah, the Son of God, who is to come into the world."

JOHN 11:27

As Martha and Mary were mourning their brother Lazarus's death, they got news of Jesus's arrival, and Martha raced to meet him. Heartbroken, Martha acknowledged Jesus's power to heal and to even bring Lazarus back to life.

When Jesus revealed Himself as the resurrection and the life, Martha responded with an unreserved confession of faith. It echoes Simon Peter's confession when he says to Jesus, "You are the Messiah, the Son of the living God" (Matthew 16:16). In her faith and trust, Martha believed it would never be too late for God to act. Her confidence in Jesus was boundless and reminds us that in Christ all things are possible.

Her faith told her something more: that this promised Messiah was not just a man but was in some mysterious way participating in the actual life of God Himself.

MARY, MOTHER OF JESUS

For the Mighty One has done great things for me—
holy is his name.

LUKE 1:49

After Gabriel delivered the news to Mary that she would give birth to the Savior of the world, she sang of the goodness of God. Her focus wasn't on the baby yet to come but on the faithfulness of God, who had sent her the heavenly assignment. We would all understand if she felt overwhelmed by the magnitude of her task, but instead she spoke with confidence in His mercy, remembering both the actions she had seen and the promises yet to be fulfilled. Mary declared, "He has performed mighty deeds" (Luke 1:51) and "filled the hungry with good things" (Luke 1:53).

In our moments of uncertainty, we can also join the chorus proclaiming God's faithfulness.

Mary would never see the world the same way again, and she didn't keep this knowledge to herself: she proclaimed it.

THE MIGHTY ONE HAS DONE GREAT THINGS FOR ME

MARY, MOTHER OF JESUS, AND A REQUEST

His mother said to the servants,
"Do whatever he tells you."

JOHN 2:5

Mary was instrumental in Jesus's first public display of miraculous power. Mary and Jesus, along with His disciples, attended a wedding in Cana. When the wine ran dry, Mary brought the issue to His attention. She knew what Jesus was capable of. At first, Jesus suggested it wasn't yet time for His public ministry to begin, so rather than pushing Jesus, Mary simply instructed the servants to do whatever he said. Jesus turned water into wine—wine so good that it baffled everyone.

Mary challenges us to take even our littlest needs to Jesus and do whatever He asks.

He took the next step in His ministry that day—and
came one step closer to the brutal death that would
pave the way for a lost world's salvation.

DO WHATEVER HE TELLS YOU

MARY, MOTHER OF JESUS, AND PRAYERFUL WAITING

"I am the Lord's servant," Mary answered. "May your word to me be fulfilled." Then the angel left her.

LUKE 1:38

After Jesus was crucified, resurrected, and ascended to heaven from the Mount of Olives, the disciples returned to Jerusalem and the upper room where they had gathered before. Mary joined them in prayer. Together, they waited for the gift of the Holy Spirit. This was exactly the kind of prayer Mary had modeled her whole life. Her entire relationship with God had been one of waiting for His promises to be fulfilled, even when they seemed impossible by human standards. Who better than she to model for Jesus's disciples and us what true, prayerful waiting looks like?

Mary's life, grounded in prayer and patience, showed the early Christians that the only road to lasting joy was often through sorrow and prayerful waiting for God.

MAY YOUR WORD

TO ME BE

FULFILLED

MARY MAGDALENE

So if the Son sets you free, you will be free indeed.

JOHN 8:36

Mary Magdalene was an important part of Jesus's life, yet the Gospel of Luke shares an explosive detail: this was the Mary from whom seven demons had come out (Luke 8:2). Jesus said the one who had experienced the greatest forgiveness would love the most, and Mary appears to have loved Jesus with passionate devotion.

In all four Gospels, Mary Magdalene was a witness to the Crucifixion, and in the Gospel of John she was the first witness to the miracle of the Resurrection. Mary Magdalene reminds us that no one is beyond God's healing and redemption.

From the very beginning, He saw the women who followed Him
as beloved children of God who deserved a chance
to learn about and follow their Heavenly Father.

IF THE SON SETS YOU *Free*, YOU WILL BE FREE INDEED

MARY MAGDALENE'S NAME FOR JESUS

Jesus said to her, "Mary."
She turned toward him and cried out in Aramaic,
"Rabboni!" (which means "Teacher")

JOHN 20:16

In the Bible, the use of a name is the single most powerful way to establish connection. To be known and seen by God is to be loved unconditionally, and that is what Mary Magdalene encountered at Jesus's tomb. When she peeked inside, she saw two angels who asked her why she was crying. She told them that Jesus's body was missing, but then she turned around and saw Jesus. At first, she didn't recognize Him until He spoke her name. That's when Mary Magdalene cried out, "Rabonni!"

"Rabboni" was a title of affection—like saying, "my dear teacher." We, too, can cry out to Jesus as our dear teacher, savior, and friend.

Jesus needs to be our teacher, one with whom
we actually have a two-way relationship.

MARY MAGDALENE'S ANNOUNCEMENT

Mary Magdalene went to the disciples with the news: "I have seen the Lord!" And she told them that he had said these things to her.

JOHN 20:18

When Mary Magdalene discovered an empty tomb on the first Easter morning, she ran to tell the disciples. The shell-shocked Peter and John raced to inspect the open tomb and then returned home, while Mary Magdalene stayed behind, sobbing by herself. Then the resurrected Jesus greeted her and instructed her to go tell the other disciples.

Mary Magdalene shared with them the incredible news: "I have seen the Lord!" (John 20:18). As a woman, she was entrusted with the greatest news of all time—the resurrection of Jesus Christ—and the world has never been the same. We, too, are entrusted to share this incredible news everywhere we go.

There's an ancient Christian tradition that calls Mary the "apostle to the apostles," because she was the one who brought the news of the Resurrection to them.

THE ACCUSED WOMAN

"No one, sir," she said.
"Then neither do I condemn you," Jesus declared.
"Go now and leave your life of sin."

JOHN 8:11

A woman accused of adultery was dragged before Jesus as He was teaching in the Temple courts. The religious leaders demanded to know if they should stone the woman according to the law. Rather than take the bait, Jesus responded, "Let any one of you who is without sin be the first to throw a stone at her" (John 8:7). He turned the crowd's phony piety against them. One by one they disappeared until Jesus and the woman remained. Then Jesus told her He didn't condemn her either—she should go free and sin no more.

Jesus gave her dignity and a second chance, as He does for us every single one of us.

Jesus specifically lovingly confronted the woman
and redirected her into a new life.

GO NOW *and* LEAVE YOUR LIFE *of* SIN

THE SAMARITAN WOMAN

"Sir," the woman said, "you have nothing to draw with and the well is deep. Where can you get this living water?"

JOHN 4:11

The longest conversation Jesus had with any woman in the Bible was with the Samaritan woman at the well. When Jesus, a Jewish man, asked her for a drink of water, the woman was shocked that He would even speak to her. Jesus responded that if she truly knew who she was speaking to, she'd have asked him for water—and He'd serve her living water. Brimming with curiosity, the Samaritan woman humbly asked about this water, and in response Jesus revealed Himself as the living water—both to her and to us today.

The woman became the first evangelist to the Samaritan people, leading many to believe in Jesus and teaching us that we can share the good news to anyone, anywhere, anytime.

Sometimes we experience the same thing when we meet Jesus at the well. For us, that means coming to the pages of Scripture or in humble prayer and sitting with Him there.

Where can you get this living water?

THE WIDOW OF NAIN

***When the Lord saw her, his heart went out to her
and he said, "Don't cry."***

LUKE 7:13

When Jesus and His disciples approached the town of Nain, they encountered a woman in a devastating situation walking along in a funeral procession. She had no husband and had lost her only son—likely the only person who could provide for her and watch over her. Jesus saw this woman and His heart went out to her. He said, "Don't cry" (Luke 7:13). Then Jesus went up and touched the coffin, and the young man came back to life.

Not only do we see a death-defying miracle, but we also see Jesus's deep kindness for women everywhere—including us—who face hard seasons of sorrow and distress.

Christ was simply so moved that He reached out to this woman and turned her nightmare into something beyond her wildest dreams.

WHEN THE LORD SAW HER, HIS HEART WENT OUT TO HER

THE WIDOW AND HER OFFERING

They all gave out of their wealth; but she, out of her poverty, put in everything—all she had to live on."

MARK 12:44

Sitting near the temple offering, Jesus and the disciples watched as people paraded their lavish donations for everyone to see. Meanwhile, a humble widow approached the offering box with two tiny coins. Though she offered the least, she became the biggest hero.

Jesus explained to His disciples that while everyone else gave out of their abundance, this woman had given out of her extreme lack. The widow, so anonymous that we don't even know her name, was the one Christ chose to use to reveal real generosity. She challenges us to ponder on the true purpose of giving.

This widow, so anonymous that we don't even know her name, is the one Christ chose to show us real giving.

THE MOTHER-IN-LAW OF PETER

So he went to her, took her hand, and helped her up.
The fever left her and she began to wait on them.

MARK 1:31

After Jesus taught on the Sabbath, He traveled to one of His disciples' homes. There, Peter's mother-in-law was in bed with a high fever. Seeing this ailment, Jesus didn't hesitate and did three things: He went to her, took her hand, and helped her up (Mark 1:31). Instantly, the woman was healed and responded by serving Jesus and the disciples.

Not only does this woman give us a powerful example of how to respond to the healing work of God in our lives, but she also reminds us that when we're hurting, Jesus is ready to come to us, take us by the hand, and help us back up.

Throughout the New Testament, women are at the center of so many of Jesus's lessons.

SHE BEGAN TO WAIT ON THEM

THE WOMAN WHO COULDN'T WALK

When Jesus saw her, he called her forward and said to her,
"Woman, you are set free from your infirmity."

LUKE 13:12

Jesus was teaching on the Sabbath when He encountered a woman who had been crippled for eighteen years and been unable to stand all those years. Yet "Jesus saw her" (Luke 13:12).

How many people had probably looked away from this woman, avoiding eye contact and conversation? Remember, many people in that time viewed sickness as a punishment for sin. Jesus looked directly at her and called her to Him: "Woman, you are set free from your infirmity." Then He touched her and immediately she straightened up and started praising God! She reminds us that Jesus won't let anything get in the way of Him bringing healing to us.

Imagine her sheer joy. Not only had Jesus Himself seen her
and called her to Him in front of everyone in the synagogue, but
He had set her free!

WOMEN'S HEALING ON THE SABBATH

When he said this, all his opponents were humiliated, but the people were delighted with all the wonderful things he was doing.

LUKE 13:17

Jesus performed many of His healings on the Sabbath, which made Him deeply unpopular with many of the religious leaders of the day. Jesus was about His father's business—even if that meant breaking through religious barriers. This was true of both the mother-in-law of Peter and the woman who couldn't walk.

The people were delighted, but the indignant leaders criticized Him. In response, Jesus challenged by asking why they'd happily water animals on the Sabbath but harshly refuse to free a woman from years of pain and anguish. Women revealed one of Jesus's most critical lessons: you can't choose legalistic rules over people and over real lives that need care and redemption.

The leader of the synagogue was "indignant" that Jesus had healed someone on the Sabbath. How dare He?

THE WOMAN WHO REACHED

Immediately her bleeding stopped and she felt in her body that she was freed from her suffering.

MARK 5:29

Jesus encounters a woman whose name we'll never know. She had suffered with bleeding for twelve long years. According to custom, she could not worship in a temple, and many would have considered her unclean. This likely meant she couldn't touch the people she loved most: her own family and friends. She had heard reports of Jesus's healings (Mark 5:27), and the ailing woman worked her way close enough to reach out and touch the hem of the miracle worker.

With a brush of her fingers, "Immediately her bleeding stopped and she felt in her body that she was freed from her suffering" (Mark 5:29). Indeed, when we reach toward Jesus, everything can change in an instant.

After more than a decade of suffering, bad news, and financial ruin, she was finally free, healed in an instant—all because she dared reach out to Him for help when every earthly avenue had ended in nothing but loss and despair.

SHE WAS *Freed* FROM HER SUFFERING

THE WOMAN WHO TOLD THE WHOLE TRUTH

*Then he said to her, "Daughter,
your faith has healed you. Go in peace."*

LUKE 8:48

When the woman who had bled for a dozen years reached for the hem of Jesus's clothing, she was healed. But that's not the end of the story; Jesus knew what had happened and asked who had touched him.

The woman approached Jesus trembling with fear, fell before Him, and told Him the whole truth (Mark 5:33). Only He could have known in that moment just how much she had suffered or how she had courageously approached him. In all the Gospel accounts, He called her "Daughter" and said her faith had healed her. Like this woman, Jesus invites us to bring the whole truth, experience healing, and go in peace.

*Jesus didn't see women as helpless. He looked at the bleeding woman
and saw a woman of remarkable faith, courage, and agency.
He saw a proud daughter of Israel.*

THE DAUGHTER OF JAIRUS

But he took her by the hand and said,
"My child, get up!"

LUKE 8:54

Jairus threw himself at Jesus's feet, pleading for his daughter's life. But news soon arrived of her death, and Jesus responded, "Don't be afraid; just believe, and she will be healed" (Luke 8:50). Jesus traveled to the girl's home, took her by the hand, and instructed her to get up.

Imagine what that moment must have been like for this girl, to suddenly open her eyes to find herself surrounded by people grieving her death . . . and to look into the eyes of the man who'd just brought her back to life. The girl who died was empowered by Christ to stand on her own—and He does the same for us.

She was the living embodiment of a miracle,
a story she and her family would carry for life,
and a reminder to us of God's remarkable power.

THE PROVERBS 31 WOMAN

She is clothed with strength and dignity;
she can laugh at the days to come.

PROVERBS 31:25

Throughout the book of Proverbs, wisdom is personified as a woman. We should not be surprised that the final chapter of Proverbs is a poem about a bold and wise woman in action. She trades, invests, manages, and makes business deals. She also brings honor to her home, watches out for everyone under her care, and shows compassion to all. She's hardworking and a good steward of her resources.

Proverbs 31 embodies wisdom in action and becomes an example to us all that with God's help we may live out these words: "She is clothed with strength and dignity; she can laugh at the days to come" (Proverbs 31:25).

Anyone who thinks the women of either the Old or New Testament were simply side notes hasn't been paying attention. The woman described in Proverbs 31 is the perfect example.

ABOUT THE AUTHOR

SHANNON BREAM is the anchor of Fox News Channel's *FOX News Sunday.* She is the author of the #1 *New York Times* bestsellers *The Women of the Bible Speak* and *The Mothers and Daughters of the Bible Speak.* She is chief legal correspondent for the network and host of *Livin' with Bream,* a Fox News Radio podcast. Shannon has anchored a wide variety of coverage for high profile stories, including the 2016 presidential election, James Comey's 2017 Congressional testimony, and key Supreme Court decisions such as Obergefell and the Defense of Marriage Act. She earned a Juris Doctorate with honors from Florida State University College of Law and lives in Washington, DC.

ABOUT THE ILLUSTRATOR

HAZEL KARKARIA is a graphic designer and lettering artist based in India. Apart from a deep love for typography, she is immensely passionate about the natural world and the realm of food and tries to weave these themes into her work.

FROM SHANNON BREAM,
#1 *NEW YORK TIMES* BESTSELLING AUTHOR

THE WOMEN OF THE BIBLE SPEAK COLORING BOOK

With this coloring and contemplation companion to the #1 *New York Times* bestselling phenomenon *The Women of the Bible Speak*, spend time with the women of the Bible, including Mary, Ruth, and Sarah, through thirty-six Bible verses to color and cherish. Experience the words of God and the beautifully designed illustrations that bring these verses to life. Thoughtful explanations also offer the biblical context for each verse.

Harper Design
An *Imprint of Harper Collins Publishers*
www.hc.com

With 36 black-and-white illustrations

Illustrations by Hazel Karkaria

FOX NEWS books

RELIGION/ART

ISBN 978-0-06-330740-7

51799

EAN

9 780063 307407

USA $17.99 / $21.99 CAN

0223